Written and Illustrated by
Sean Laven

Where did all the Playgrounds go?

Dedicated to
all of the little ones
affected by Covid-19.

Today is the day
I'll go and **play,**

I see **no** reason
to stay away.

The sun is **out,**
the clouds are gone,

Now it's time to ask my **MOM.**

Oh Mom Oh Mom
can we go?

You said real soon,

I checked for snow.

The Snow's all gone,
the sun is out.

Can we please go run about?

My son
my son,
we can not go.

Yes I saw **you** checked for **snow**.

And yes

I see the **sun** is out.

But we still *can't* go run **about**.

The swings have to be **cleaned**

and so does the pool.

And Grandma's

and Grandpa's and Auntie's too.

These places **we** go
all have to be **cleaned,**
because of something called COVID-19.

The
Playgrounds
are **sick.**

And so
is the

Zoo.

Just like when you sneeze;

Ahh Ahhh

Ahhhhh

CHOOOOO!

So we

wash

our

hands.

And we wear

a mask.

And we **always** read the Playground **facts.**

Of **what** to do and **when** to go, even though there is no **snow.**

Now it's **ok** Son,

don't be **mad**.

But **if** you are a little **sad**...

Remember that the **Sun** is out,

and **Soon** enough we'll run about.

CPSIA information can be obtained
at www.ICGtesting.com
Printed in the USA
LVHW072001120720
660447LV00003BA/7